Special Thanks to Jack Bursk, Roman Volsky, the Library of Congress, and all those who strive to better themselves.

"A good example is the best Sermon."

Benjamin Franklin

Mind Your Manners!

George Washington's Rules of Civility

with Observations by James Henry II

Dedicated to Good Taste

Visit the website at
www.RulesofCivility.com

Library of Congress Cataloging in Publication Data
Henry II, James
    Mind Your Manners!
    George Washington's Manners Manual
    2nd Edition
ISBN 978-0-9817047-2-2
1. Civility. 2. Good Taste. 3. Etiquette
Serious Literature
Library of Congress Control Number: 2010910009
© James Henry 2010

Culturally Conscious Publishing

Flint Hill, Virginia

Introduction

In the spirit of our Founding Fathers, I bring you the one hundred and ten rules that guided the life of George Washington, our nation's first president. In a day when being crude, crass, and offensive is in vogue, these rules speak to a different impulse. They remind us that beyond our desire for the immediate gratification of every whim there are other people with their own sensibilities and notions of dignity. They remind us of the early days of this country when being civil to friend and foe alike was not only good manners but a sign of one's worth.

Since the sixties, many have striven to release themselves from conformist conventions, a worthy pursuit when done in good conscience But today many feel trapped in a society of self-centered, self-interested individuals lacking consideration for their companions in this thing called life. Washington would likely view our society as uncouth and unkind. His upbringing taught him that mutual respect toward one another builds strong individual character, strong communities, and a strong society.

In the middle ages, manners manuals were quite popular. Dozens of such instructional books can be found in the Library of Congress. These books outlined proper conduct from the dinner table, to the bathroom, to courtly encounters. In colonial America many up and coming gentlemen from the land-holding class looked up to England and Europe, eagerly consuming etiquette books. They sought to emulate the established mainland families, and manuals such as these were useful tools. One such manual found its way into the lessons of a colonial American boy striving to become a Virginia gentleman.

The precise origins of the text are not fully known, but professional guesswork has shed much light on the matter. The late Moncure D. Conway traced the maxims to a 16th century Jesuit-compiled treatise entitled "Bienséance de la Conversation entre les Homme" and written in the year 1595. It was based on manuals from the middle ages, most probably the Italian *Galeteo*. The text was translated into English in 1640, allegedly by the eight-year-old child Francis Hawkin, but more than likely he owes credit to his ambitious father. Finally some unknown person edited and presented the text to the young Washington, probably not yet 16, who wrote them into his school notes as a part of his education.

The Rules of Civility served as the moral compass for George Washington. The impact these maxims had on his life was evident from the beginning. At age 17 he was hired as a surveyor by Lord Fairfax of Virginia. Attending Fairfax's "Greenway Court" gave George his first opportunity to practice these rules. As a young man he was known for his good character and social graces, and as a mature planter, general, and president, his dignified and gracious demeanor continued to impress everyone who came into contact with him. His attention to civility and humility was pivotal to his rise in influence and overall success.

The rules that helped mold Washington still serve as a model for today. Although not every maxim is applicable to modern society, each and every one allows us to step back and examine how our actions are perceived by and affect those around us. The Rules focus on outward behavior: postures, placements, and comments that gradually permeate the individual to his inner core. We are not only what we eat, but what we think, say, and do. A well-mannered and balanced individual will be mindful of others and himself. As Franklin said, "Ceremony is not Civility; nor Civility Ceremony." To be good to others is to be good to ourselves. Civility produces better individuals and therefore a better civilization.

Manners and etiquette may be far from the interests of today's youth, but the values they instill are ripe for a revival. Resolving ourselves to be kind and civil to our countrymen, in the manner of our preeminent first president, is an ethic worth embracing in these rough and ready times.

Each page of this edition of The Rules of Civility includes an image, the original rule, in Washington's boyhood grammar, and an up-to-date observation to better convey these maxims to the "busy" modern-day reader.

Rule 1

Every Action done in Company ought to be with Some Sign of Respect to those that are Present.

George Washington

Leave a better impression of yourself on your companions than that of your boot on their face.

James Henry

Rule 2

*W*hen in Company, put not your Hands to any Part of the Body, not usually Discovered.

George Washington

*F*ishing for one's privates rarely should be done in public.

James Henry

Rule 3

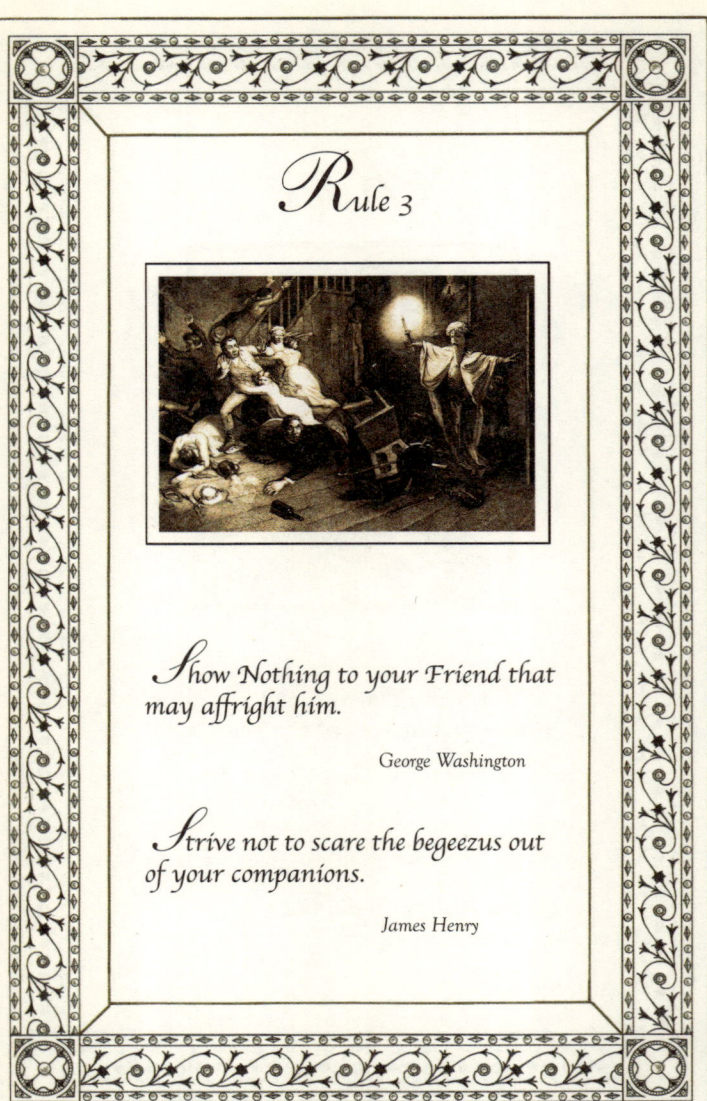

*S*how Nothing to your Friend that may affright him.

George Washington

*S*trive not to scare the begeezus out of your companions.

James Henry

Rule 4

In the Presence of Others Sing not to yourself with a humming Noise, nor Drum with your Fingers or Feet.

George Washington

The sweetness of your singing may be in your mind only, and it would be best to keep it there.

James Henry

Rule 5

If You Cough, Sneeze, Sigh, or Yawn, do it not Loud but Privately; and Speak not in your Yawning, but put Your handkerchief or Hand before your face and turn aside.

George Washington

Company should be spared the sight of the interior of your facial cavity.

James Henry

Rule 6

*S*leep not when others Speak, Sit not when others stand, Speak not when you Should hold your Peace, walk not on when others Stop.

George Washington

*W*hen others approach to greet you, make every effort to get off your ass.

James Henry

Rule 7

$\mathcal{P}$ut not off your Clothes in the presence of Others, nor go out your Chamber half Drest.

George Washington

$\mathcal{B}$efore going nude, be sure to set the mood.

James Henry

Rule 8

*A*t Play and at Fire it's Good manners to Give Place to the last Comer, and affect not to Speak Louder than Ordinary.

George Washington

*I*t is not in good taste to shout or swing fire pokers at your companions.

James Henry

Rule 9

*S*pit not in the Fire, nor Stoop low before it neither Put your Hands into the Flames to warm them, nor Set your Feet upon the Fire especially if there be meat before it.

George Washington

*W*hile seated by fire, mind the flames and watch your dress, because no host enjoys a charred guest.

James Henry

Rule 10

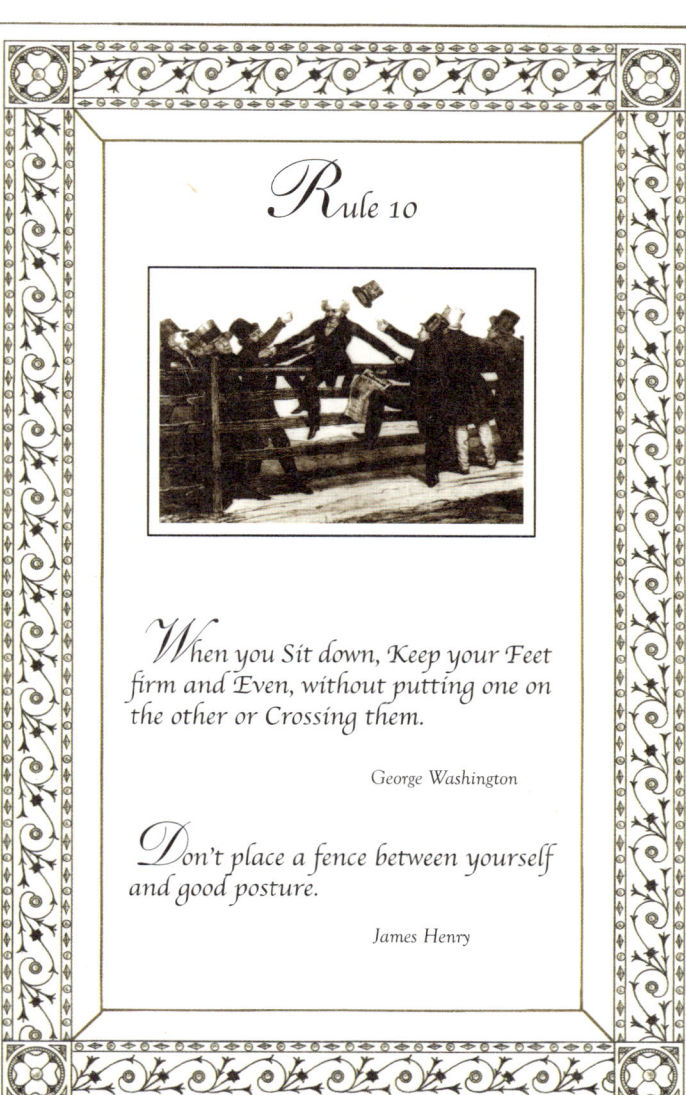

When you Sit down, Keep your Feet firm and Even, without putting one on the other or Crossing them.

George Washington

Don't place a fence between yourself and good posture.

James Henry

Rule 11

$\mathcal{S}$hift not yourself in the Sight of others nor Gnaw your nails.

George Washington

$\mathcal{L}$oosen the body at the gym or under the sheets.

James Henry

Rule 12

Shake not the head, Feet, or Legs. Roll not the Eyes lift not one eyebrow higher than the other wry not the mouth, and bedew no mans face with your Spittle, by approaching too near him when you Speak.

George Washington

When speaking, be attuned to the flying fluids from your mouth. Few enjoy spitteled speech.

James Henry

Rule 13

*K*ill no Vermin as Fleas, lice, ticks etc. in the Sight of Others, if you See any filth or thick Spittle put your foot Dexterously upon it. If it be upon the Cloths of your Companions, Put it off privately, and if it be upon your own Cloths return Thanks to him who puts it off.

George Washington

*I*t is bad taste to destroy little creatures in the sight of others. If your friend has a booger or toilet paper hanging from his person, quietly inform him.

James Henry

Rule 14

Turn not your Back to others especially in Speaking, Jog not the Table or Desk on which Another reads or writes, lean not upon any one.

George Washington

Speak to others with your face rather than your behind.

James Henry

Rule 15

*K*eep your Nails clean and Short, also your Hands and Teeth Clean yet without Showing any great Concern for them.

George Washington

*S*tay neat and clean without being a queen.

James Henry

Rule 16

$\mathcal{D}$o not Puff up the Cheeks, Loll not out the tongue, rub the Hands, or beard, thrust out the lips, or bite them or keep the Lips too open or too Close.

George Washington

$\mathcal{A}$void entertaining the company with odd expressions or ostentatious facial ticks.

James Henry

Rule 17

Be no Flatterer, neither Play with any that delights not to be Play'd Withal.

George Washington

Don't play with the unplayful.

James Henry

Rule 18

*R*ead no Letters, Books, or Papers in Company but when there is a Necessity for the doing of it you must ask leave: come not near the Books or Writings of Another so as to read them unless desired or give your opinion of them unask'd. Also look not nigh when another is writing a Letter.

George Washington

*A*void reading political or pornographic material at the dinner table.

James Henry

Rule 19

Let your Countenance be pleasant but in Serious Matters Somewhat grave.

George Washington

Always project a pleasant air, even if you receive a bitter glare.

James Henry

Rule 20

$\mathcal{T}$he Gestures of the Body must be Suited to the discourse you are upon.

George Washington

$\mathcal{L}$et your body suggest what your words propose.

James Henry

Rule 21

Reproach none for their Infirmities of Nature, nor Delight to Put them that have in mind hereof.

George Washington

Don't tease freaks or unfortunate geeks.

James Henry

Rule 22

Show not yourself glad at the Misfortune of another though he were your enemy.

George Washington

Avoid open displays of glee at the troubles of your adversary.

James Henry

Rule 23

When you see a Crime punished, you may be inwardly Pleased; but always show Pity to the Suffering Offender.

George Washington

Moderate unseemly expressions of dark joy at the misfortune of others.

James Henry

Rule 24

*D*o not laugh too loud or too much at any Publick Spectacle lest you cause yourself to be laughed at.

George Washington

*T*ake no part in displays of the common rabble. Refrain from excessive dancing, drink, and babble.

James Henry

Rule 25

Superfluous Compliments and all Affectation of Ceremony are to be avoided, yet where due they are not to be Neglected.

George Washington

In the presence of fine females, few compliments are superfluous.

James Henry

Rule 26

In Pulling off your Hat to Persons of Distinction, as Noblemen, Justices, Churchmen &c make a Reverence, bowing more or less according to the Custom of the Better Breed, and Quality of the Person. Amongst your equals expect not always that they Should begin with you first, but to Pull off the Hat when there is no need is Affectation. In the Manner of Saluting and resaluting in words keep to the most usual Custom.

George Washington

To remove one's hat today is silly, unless it's for a girl who's pretty.

James Henry

Rule 27

'Tis ill manners to bid one more eminent than yourself be covered as well as not to do it to whom it's due. Likewise he that makes too much haste to Put on his hat does not well, yet he ought to Put it on at the first, or at most the Second time of being asked; now what is herein Spoken, of Qualification in behavior in Saluting, ought also to be observed in taking of Place, and Sitting down for ceremonies without Bounds is troublesome.

George Washington

Kow-towing to lords is no longer required.

James Henry

Rule 28

If any one come to Speak to you while you are Sitting Stand up tho he be your Inferior, and when you Present Seats let it be to every one according to his Degree.

George Washington

*A*void being a slothful guy and speak to people eye to eye.

James Henry

Rule 29

When you meet with one of Greater Quality than yourself, Stop, and retire especially if it be at a Door or any Straight place to give way for him to Pass.

George Washington

Don't rush to be the first through every doorway, you'll get there faster by being polite.

James Henry

Rule 30

*I*n walking the highest Place in most Countries Seems to be on the right hand therefore Place yourself on the left of him whom you desire to Honor: but if three walk together the middle Place is the most Honorable. The wall is usually given to the most worthy if two walk together.

George Washington

*T*he walking companion that can't stay in step has as much use as his weight in refuse.

James Henry

Rule 31

If any one far Surpasses others, either in age, Estate, or Merit yet would give Place to a meaner than himself in his own lodging or elsewhere the one ought not to accept it. So he on the other part should not use much earnestness nor offer it above once or twice.

George Washington

Make your offers wholesome rather than loathsome.

James Henry

Rule 32

To one that is your equal, or not much inferior, you are to give the chief Place in your Lodging and he to who 'tis offered ought at the first to refuse it but at the Second to accept though not without acknowledging his own unworthiness.

George Washington

Always offer your bed to appropriate guests even if you happen to be in it.

James Henry

Rule 33

They that are in Dignity or in office have in all places Precedency but whilst they are Young they ought to respect those that are their equals in Birth or other Qualitys, though they have no Publick charge.

George Washington

Trust-fund babies still should be polite.

James Henry

Rule 34

It is good Manners to prefer them to whom we Speak before ourselves especially if they be above us with whom in no Sort we ought to begin.

George Washington

A wise man speaks half as much as his companions.

James Henry

Rule 35

$\mathcal{L}$et your Discourse with Men of Business be Short and Comprehensive.

George Washington

$\mathcal{W}$hen the money is on the table, don't run your mouth!

James Henry

Rule 36

Artificers & Persons of low Degree ought not to use many ceremonies to Lords, or Others of high Degree but Respect and highly Honour them, and those of high Degree ought to treat them with affability & Courtesy, without Arrogance.

George Washington

In the presence of men of distinction, strive not to sully your nose brown.

James Henry

Rule 37

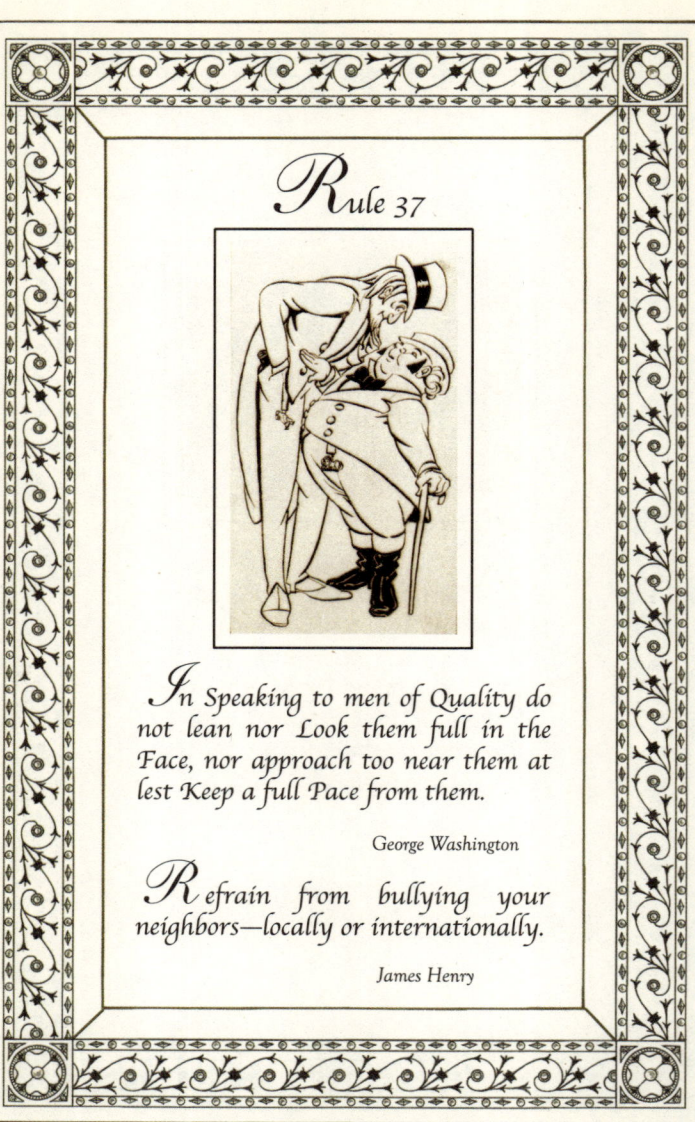

In Speaking to men of Quality do not lean nor Look them full in the Face, nor approach too near them at lest Keep a full Pace from them.

George Washington

*R*efrain from bullying your neighbors—locally or internationally.

James Henry

Rule 38

In visiting the Sick, do not Presently play the Physician if you be not Knowing therein.

George Washington

If your company falls ill due to excessive drinking, holding their hair only lightens their lesson.

James Henry

Rule 39

In writing or Speaking, give to every Person his due Title According to his Degree & the Custom of the Place.

George Washington

When speaking to persons of dignity, be respectful and mind your obscenities.

James Henry

Rule 40

Strive not with your Superiors in argument, but always Submit your Judgment to others with Modesty.

George Washington

Masters are not to be meddled with, especially ones with violent tendencies.

James Henry

Rule 41

Undertake not to Teach your equal in the art himself Proffesses; it Savours of arrogancy.

George Washington

Nobody likes a know-it-all.

James Henry

Rule 42

Let thy ceremonies in Courtesie be proper to the Dignity of his place with whom thou converse for it is absurd to act ye same with a Clown and a Prince.

George Washington

Don't wear false faces simply for social graces.

James Henry

Rule 43

*D*o not express Joy before one sick or in pain, for that contrary Passion will aggravate his Misery.

George Washington

*A*void torturing the ill with your overzealous merriment.

James Henry

Rule 44

When a man does all he can though it Succeeds not well, blame not him that did it.

George Washington

Resist tormenting the incompetent, unless they really ask for it.

James Henry

Rule 45

Being to advise or reprehend any one, consider whether it ought to be in publick or in Private; presently, or at Some other time, in what terms to do it, & in reproving Show no Sign of Cholar but do it with all Sweetness and Mildness.

George Washington

When offering up criticism, make sure your companion isn't carrying a big stick.

James Henry

Rule 46

Take all Admonitions thankfully in what Time or Place Soever given but afterwards not being culpable take a Time & Place convenient to let him know it that gave them.

George Washington

When receiving critique, even if it be blunt, receive it thankfully. Choose the proper time and place for reprisal.

James Henry

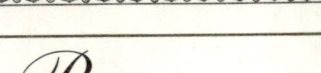
Rule 47

Mock not nor Jest at any thing of Importance. Break no Jest that are Sharp Biting and if you Deliver any thing witty and Pleasant abstain from Laughing thereat yourself.

George Washington

Avoid making jest to the detriment of others, unless it's really funny.

James Henry

Rule 48

*W*herein you reprove Another be unblamable yourself; for example is more prevalent than Precepts.

George Washington

*P*ut on your boots before your tongue becomes loose.

James Henry

Rule 49

*U*se no Reproachful Language against any one; neither Curse nor Revile.

George Washington

*D*o not curse or make racial slurs at the 7-Eleven.

James Henry

Rule 50

$\mathcal{B}$e not hasty to believe flying Reports to the Disparagement of any.

George Washington

$\mathcal{A}$s fun as gossip is to hear, always lend it a cautious ear.

James Henry

Rule 51

Wear not your Cloths, foul, ripped or Dusty but See they be Brush'd once every day at least and take heed that you approach not to any Uncleaness.

George Washington

Soiled clothing isn't stylish.

James Henry

Rule 52

In your Apparel be Modest and endeavor to accommodate Nature, rather than to procure Admiration. Keep to the Fashion of your equals Such as are Civil and orderly wit respect to Times and Places.

George Washington

Unless it's your chosen method to procure a mate, spare the public your perverse attire.

James Henry

Rule 53

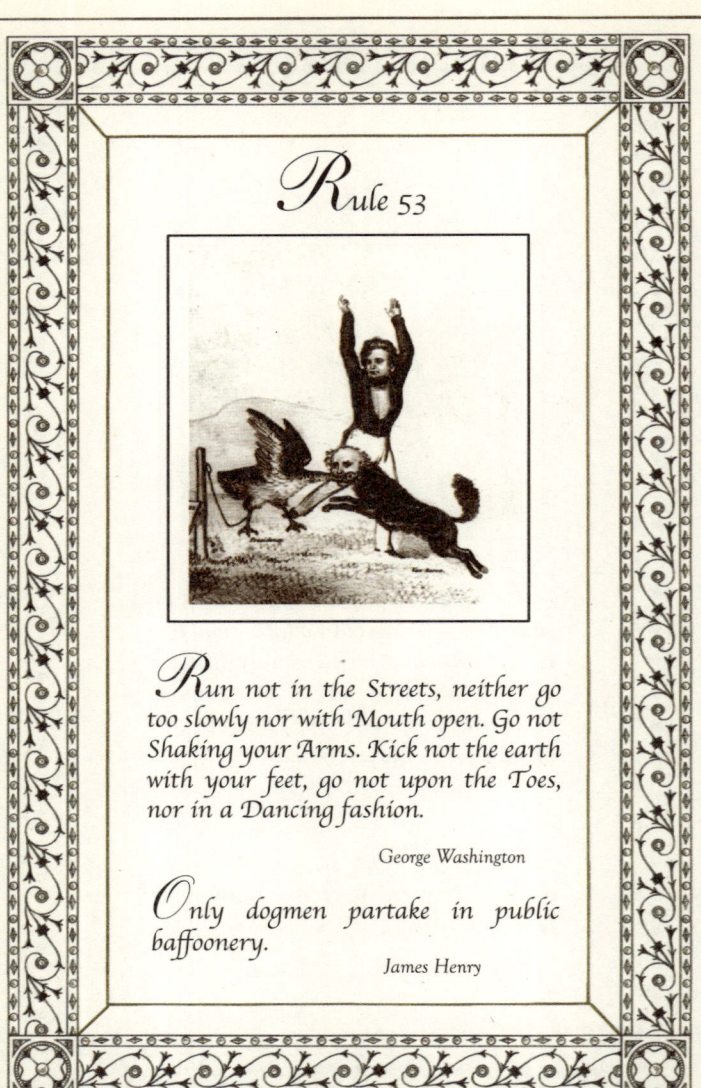

Run not in the Streets, neither go too slowly nor with Mouth open. Go not Shaking your Arms. Kick not the earth with your feet, go not upon the Toes, nor in a Dancing fashion.

George Washington

Only dogmen partake in public baffoonery.

James Henry

Rule 54

Play not the Peacock, looking every where about you, to See if you be well Deck't, if your Shoes fit well if your Stockings Sit neatly, and Cloths handsomely.

George Washington

Life is a production with many actors. Play your part with confidence, especially if you're the peacock.

James Henry

Rule 55

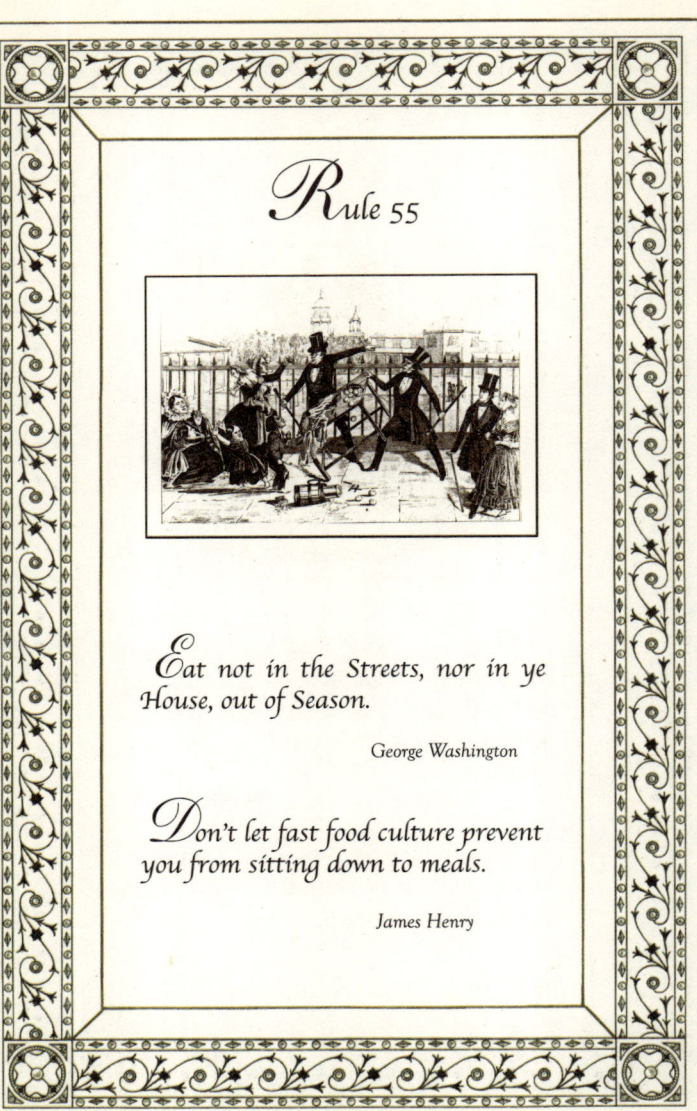

Eat not in the Streets, nor in ye House, out of Season.

George Washington

Don't let fast food culture prevent you from sitting down to meals.

James Henry

Rule 56

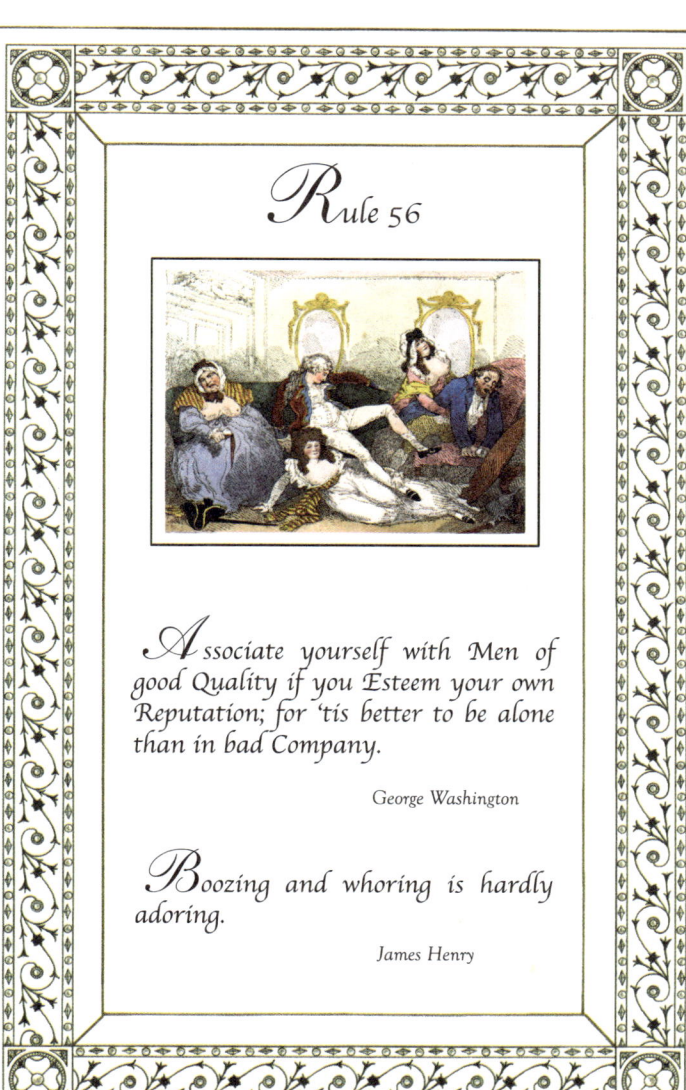

*A*ssociate yourself with Men of good Quality if you Esteem your own Reputation; for 'tis better to be alone than in bad Company.

George Washington

*B*oozing and whoring is hardly adoring.

James Henry

Rule 57

In walking up and Down in a House, only with One in Company if he be Greater than yourself, at the first give him the Right hand and Stop not till he does and be not the first that turns, and when you do turn let it be with your face towards him, if he be a Man of Great Quality, walk not with him Cheek by Joul but Somewhat behind him; but yet in Such a Manner that he may easily Speak to you.

George Washington

*W*hen walking with company, avoid stepping on their toes or ass.

James Henry

Rule 58

*L*et your Conversation be without Malice or Envy, for 'tis a Sign of a Tractable and Commendable Nature: And in all Causes of Passion admit Reason to Govern.

George Washington

*M*ind your temper and rough handling of the ladies. There's nothing like some domestic violence to shatter a pleasant silence.

James Henry

Rule 59

*N*ever express anything unbecoming, nor Act against ye Rules Moral before your inferiors.

George Washington

*P*ractice discretion on the dance floor, unless your partner requests a good spank.

James Henry

Rule 60

*B*e not immodest in urging your Friends to Discover a Secret.

George Washington

*D*on't let it be revealed if you happen upon a secret. If it be your wife's lover exiting the bedroom window, violent outbursts may be excused.

James Henry

Rule 61

*U*tter not base and frivolous things amongst grave and Learn'd Men nor very Difficult Questions or Subjects, among the Ignorant or things hard to be believed, Stuff not your Discourse with Sentences amongst your Betters nor Equals.

George Washington

*S*weet nothings form the keystone of human reproduction. Use them wisely and make them credible.

James Henry

Rule 62

Speak not of doleful Things in a Time of Mirth or at the Table; Speak not of Melancholy Things as Death and Wounds, and if others Mention them Change if you can the Discourse. Tell not your Dreams, but to your intimate Friend.

George Washington

Strive not to make your date weep over dinner.

James Henry

Rule 63

A Man ought not to value himself of his Achievements, or rare Qualities of wit; much less of his riches, Virtue or Kindred.

George Washington

Show modesty, even if know you excel others in birth, wit, wealth, virtue, accomplishments, looks, and sex life.

James Henry

Rule 64

*B*reak not a Jest where none take pleasure in mirth. Laugh not aloud, nor at all without Occasion, deride no mans Misfortune, tho' there Seem to be Some cause.

George Washington

*P*ass not the time tormenting the homeless.

James Henry

Rule 65

Speak not injurious Words neither in Jest nor Earnest Scoff at none, although they give Occasion.

George Washington

Shaking a cane in someone's direction is not a good way to win their affection.

James Henry

Rule 66

$\mathcal{B}$e not forward but friendly and Courteous; the first to Salute hear and answer & be not Pensive when it's a time to Converse.

George Washington

$\mathcal{D}$evelop the fine art of smooth talk.

James Henry

Rule 67

Detract not from others neither be excessive in Commanding.

George Washington

Refrain from striking your companions.

James Henry

Rule 68

Go not thither, where you know not, whether you Shall be Welcome or not. Give not Advice with being Ask'd & when desired do it briefly.

George Washington

Knock before entering a room or else you may get an unseemly surprise.

James Henry

Rule 69

If two contend together take not the part of either unconstrained; and be not obstinate in your own Opinion, in Things indifferent be of the Major Side.

George Washington

Be a good sheep and don't allow your views to stray from the flock.

James Henry

Rule 70

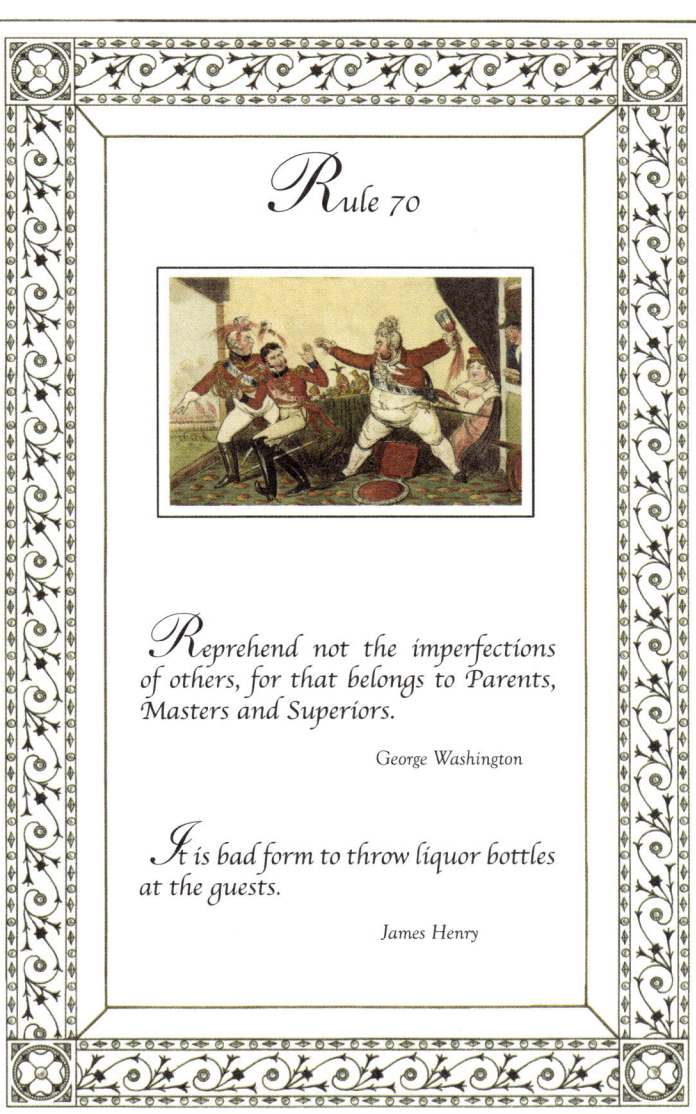

Reprehend not the imperfections of others, for that belongs to Parents, Masters and Superiors.

George Washington

It is bad form to throw liquor bottles at the guests.

James Henry

Rule 71

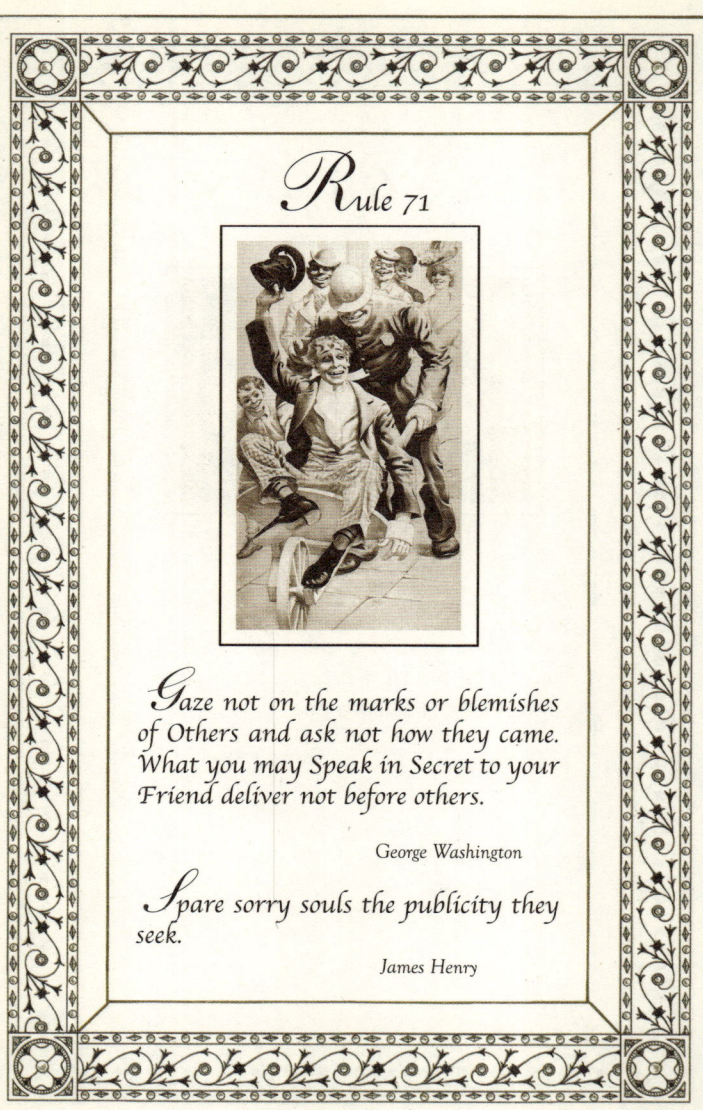

Gaze not on the marks or blemishes of Others and ask not how they came. What you may Speak in Secret to your Friend deliver not before others.

George Washington

Spare sorry souls the publicity they seek.

James Henry

Rule 72

Speak not in an unknown Tongue in Company but in your own Language and that as those of Quality do and not as ye Vulgar; Sublime matters treat Seriously.

George Washington

Speak of personal matters in private, not on your cell phone.

James Henry

Rule 73

*T*hink before you Speak. Pronounce not imperfectly nor bring out your Words too hastily but orderly & distinctly.

George Washington

*N*o one likes the sound of a stuttering fool.

James Henry

Rule 74

When Another Speaks be attentive your Self and disturb not the Audience if any hesitate in his Words help him not nor Prompt him without desired, Interrupt him not, nor Answer him till his Speech be ended.

George Washington

Always make sure your companions feel heard even if they have nothing to say.

James Henry

Rule 75

In the midst of Discourse ask not of what one treateth but if you Perceive any Stop because of your coming you may well intreat him gently to Proceed: If a Person of Quality comes in while your Conversing it's handsome to Repeat what was said before.

George Washington

While you shouldn't ask people to repeat themselves, it is good taste to do so with newcomers.

James Henry

Rule 76

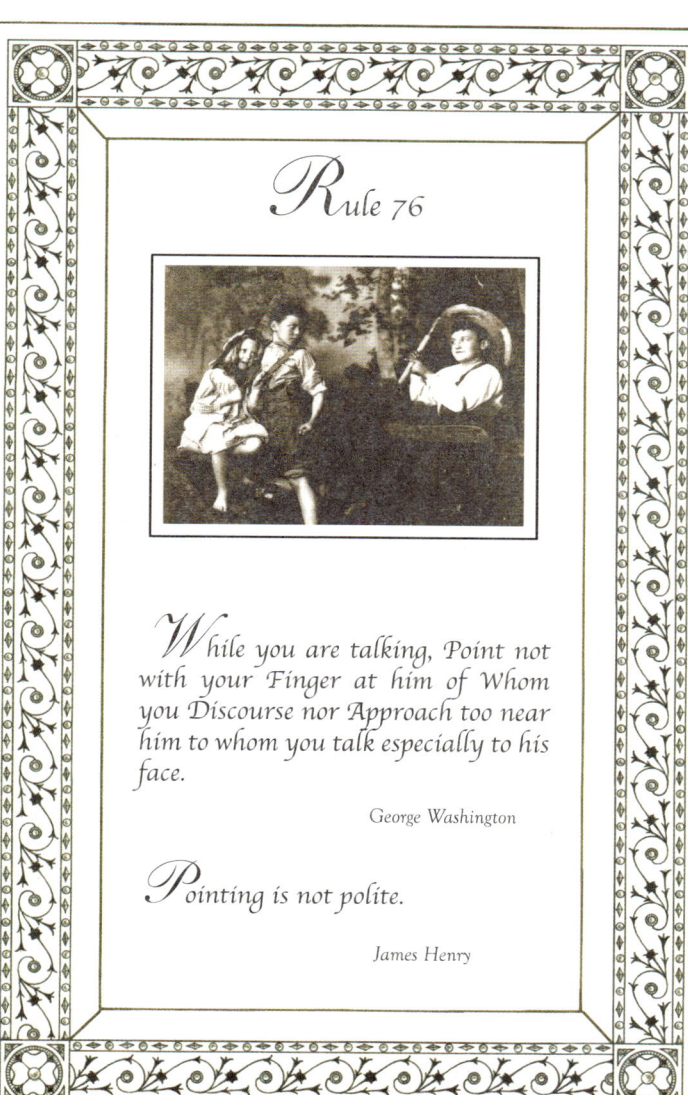

While you are talking, Point not with your Finger at him of Whom you Discourse nor Approach too near him to whom you talk especially to his face.

George Washington

Pointing is not polite.

James Henry

Rule 77

Treat with men at fit Times about Business & Whisper not in the Company of Others.

George Washington

Foster a keen awareness of when to shut up.

James Henry

Rule 78

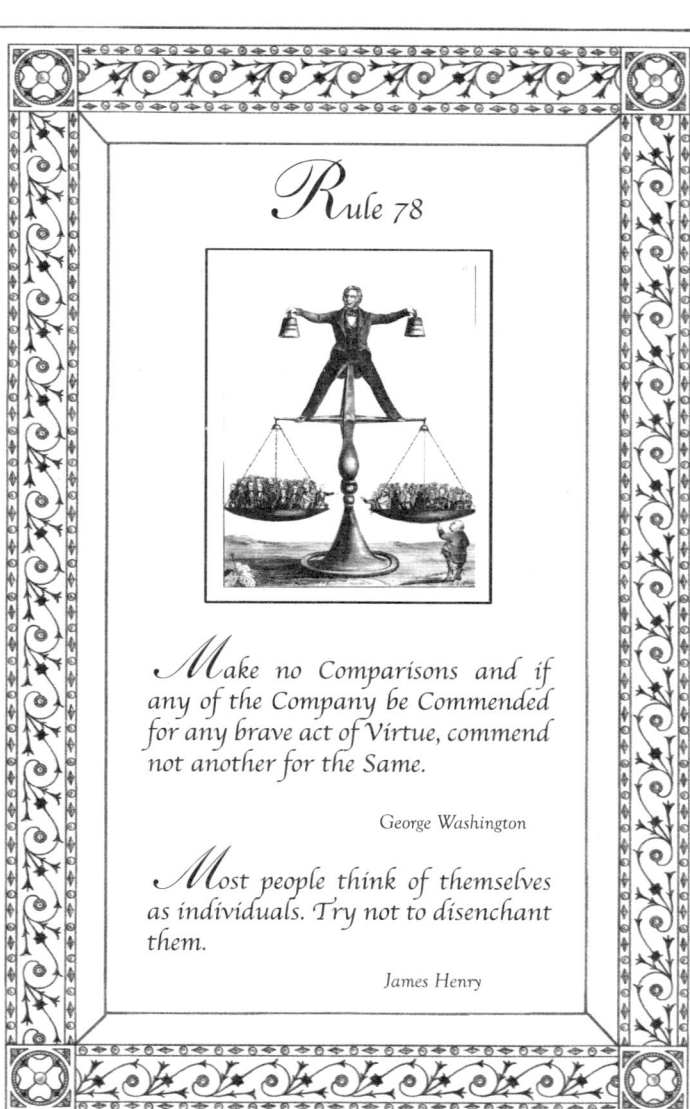

Make no Comparisons and if any of the Company be Commended for any brave act of Virtue, commend not another for the Same.

George Washington

Most people think of themselves as individuals. Try not to disenchant them.

James Henry

Rule 79

Be not apt to relate News if you know not the truth thereof. In Discoursing of things you Have heard Name not your Author always A Secret Discover not.

George Washington

Don't believe everything you read or hear.

James Henry

Rule 80

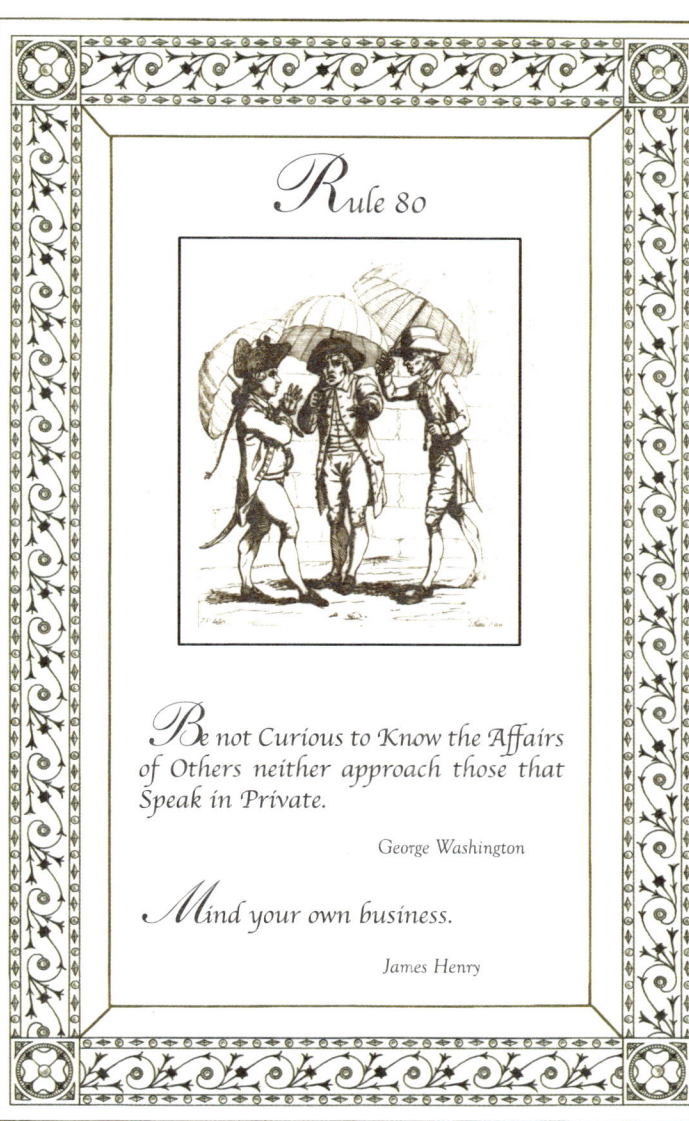

Be not Curious to Know the Affairs of Others neither approach those that Speak in Private.

George Washington

Mind your own business.

James Henry

Rule 81

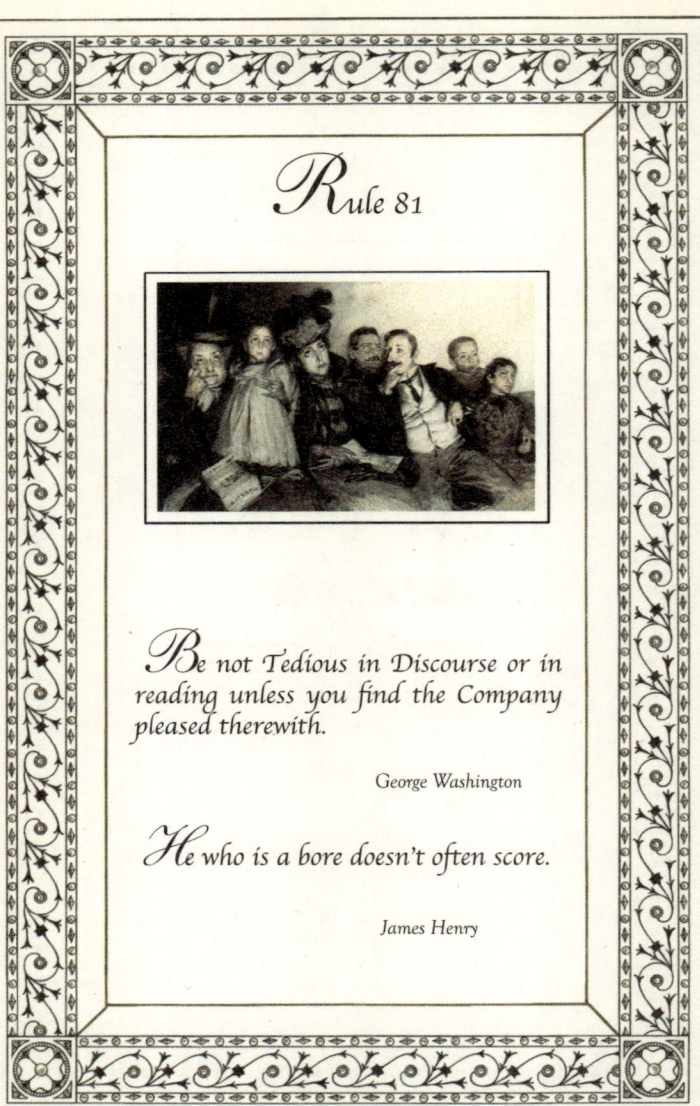

Be not Tedious in Discourse or in reading unless you find the Company pleased therewith.

George Washington

He who is a bore doesn't often score.

James Henry

Rule 82

Undertake not what you cannot Perform but be Careful to keep your Promise.

George Washington

When your promises are kept to a few, more people can count on you.

James Henry

Rule 83

When you deliver a matter do it without Passion & with Discretion, however mean ye Person be you do it too.

George Washington

Always be professional, even when your boss reveals he is an ass.

James Henry

Rule 84

*W*hen your Superiors talk to any Body hearken not neither Speak nor Laugh.

George Washington

*D*on't come-a-knocking when the bosses are-a-talking.

James Henry

Rule 85

In Company of these of Higher Quality than yourself Speak not till you are ask'd a Question then Stand upright, put of your Hat & Answer in few words.

George Washington

Brevity and clarity are the key to persuasive speaking.

James Henry

Rule 86

In Disputes, be not So Desirous to Overcome as not to give Liberty to each one to deliver his Opinion and Submit to ye Judgment of ye Major Part especially if they are Judges of the Dispute.

George Washington

*A*dmit nothing, deny everything, and be friendly with the Judge.

James Henry

Rule 87

$\mathcal{L}$et thy carriage be such as becomes a Man Grave Settled and attentive to that which is spoken. Contradict not at every turn what others Say.

George Washington

$\mathcal{B}$e an agreeable chap and don't piss off your companions.

James Henry

Rule 88

Be not tedious in Discourse, make not many Digressions, nor repeat often the Same manner of Discourse.

George Washington

*K*eep your nasty habits to yourself.

James Henry

Rule 89

*S*peak not Evil of the absent, for it is unjust.

George Washington

*S*pread not smack, for it will surely come back.

James Henry

Rule 90

Being Set at meat, Scratch not neither Spit Cough or blow your Nose except there's a Necessity for it.

George Washington

When dining, do not interject buggers into the conversation.

James Henry

Rule 91

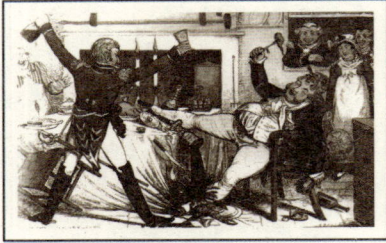

*M*ake no Show of taking great Delight in your Victuals, Feed not with Greediness; cut your Bread with a Knife, lean not on the Table neither find fault with what you Eat.

George Washington

*M*aintain composure at the table, this includes violent outbursts fueled by alcohol.

James Henry

Rule 92

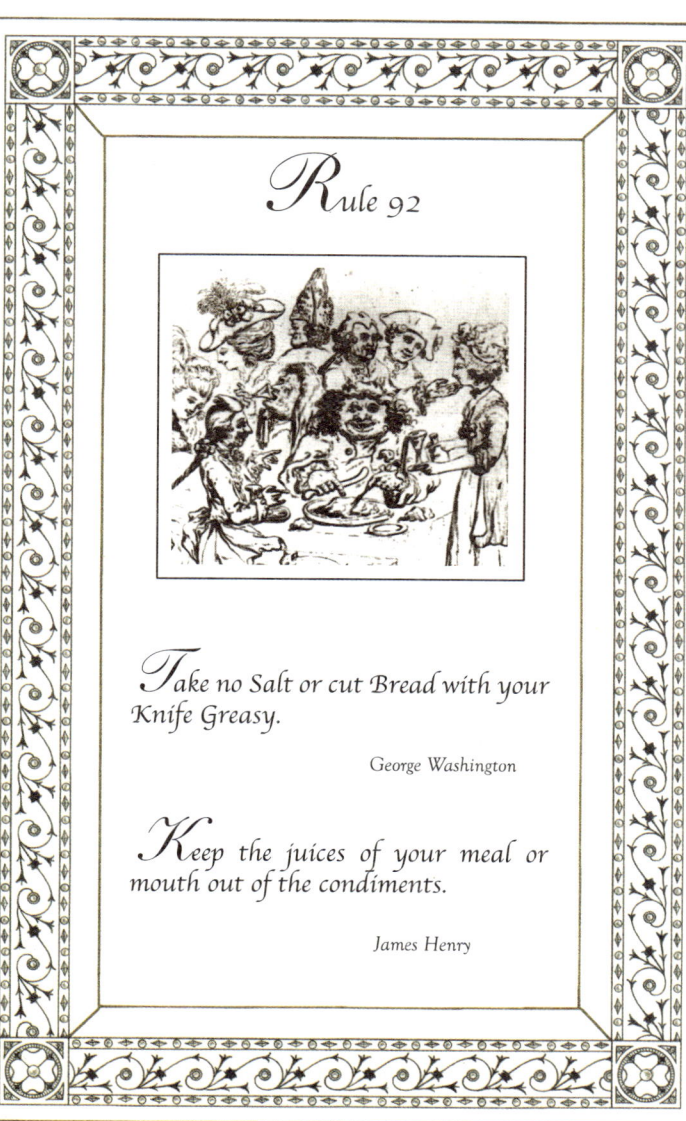

*T*ake no Salt or cut Bread with your Knife Greasy.

George Washington

*K*eep the juices of your meal or mouth out of the condiments.

James Henry

Rule 93

Entertaining any one at the table, it is decent to present him with meat; Undertake not to help others undesired by ye Master.

George Washington

Always make sure your guests are fed first... even if they are fat.

James Henry

Rule 94

If you Soak bread in the Sauce let it be no more than what you put in your Mouth at a time and blow not your broth at Table but Stay till Cools of it Self.

George Washington

While waiting for your soup to cool, don't allow your temper to boil over.

James Henry

Rule 95

$\mathcal{P}$ut not your meat to your Mouth with your Knife in your hand neither Spit forth the Stones of any fruit Pie upon a Dish nor Cast anything under the table.

George Washington

$\mathcal{W}$hen dining on shrunken heads, always remember to use a knife and fork.

James Henry

Rule 96

It's unbecoming to Stoop much to ones Meat Keep your Fingers clean & when foul wipe them on a Corner of your Table Napkin.

George Washington

Refrain from eating like a hog or you'll resemble one.

James Henry

Rule 97

Put not another bit into your Mouth til the former be Swallowed let not your Morsels be too big for the Gowls.

George Washington

Eat with ease rather than stuffing your chops.

James Henry

Rule 98

𝒟rink not nor talk with your mouth full neither Gaze about you while you are Drinking.

George Washington

𝒮eek no attention nor be rash when you're totally trashed.

James Henry

Rule 99

$\mathcal{D}$rink not too leisurely nor yet too hastily. Before and after Drinking, wipe your Lip's breath not then or Ever with too Great a Noise, for it's uncivil.

George Washington

$\mathcal{B}$e not a sloppy drunk.

James Henry

Rule 100

Cleanse not your teeth with the Table Cloth Napkin, Fork, or Knife; but if Others do it, let it be done with a Pick Tooth.

George Washington

Avoid too vigorous a public tooth picking.

James Henry

Rule 101

Rinse not your Mouth in the Presence of Others.

George Washington

Refrain from gurgling around the guests.

James Henry

Rule 102

It is out of use to call upon the Company often to Eat nor need you Drink to others every Time you Drink.

George Washington

Drunk shouting at passers by, in the book of etiquette, doesn't fly.

James Henry

Rule 103

In the Company of your Betters be not longer in eating than they are. Lay not your Arm but only your hand upon the table.

George Washington

By lagging in eating you drag on the evening.

James Henry

Rule 104

It belongs to ye Chiefest in Company to unfold his Napkin and fall to Meat first, But he ought then to Begin in time & to Dispatch with Dexterity that ye Slowest may have time allowed him.

George Washington

*A*lways allow the your companions to dig in first.

James Henry

Rule 105

Be not Angry at Table whatever happens & if you have reason to be so, Show it not; put on a Cheerful Countenance especially if there be Strangers, for Good Humor makes one Dish of Meat a Feast.

George Washington

It is always preferable to over schmooze it than to simply lose it.

James Henry

Rule 106

*S*et not yourself at ye upper of ye Table but if it be your Due or that ye master of ye house will have it So, Contend not, least you Should Trouble ye Company.

George Washington

*D*on't throw a fit over where you're asked to sit.

James Henry

Rule 107

If others talk at the Table, be attentive but talk not with Meat in your Mouth.

George Washington

No one takes interest in how well you chew your food.

James Henry

Rule 108

When you Speak of God or his Attributes, let it be Seriously & with Reverence. Honour & Obey your Natural Parents although they be Poor.

George Washington

Never utter the name of big G contemptuously.

James Henry

Rule 109

$\mathcal{L}$et your Recreations be Manfull not Sinful.

George Washington

$\mathcal{T}$ake pleasure in manly pursuits, granted they're not prostitutes.

James Henry

Rule 110

*L*abor to keep alive in your Breast that Little Spark of Celestial fire Called Conscience.

George Washington

*S*trive not to be better than your neighbor, but better than yourself.

James Henry

Notes on Civility

Notes on Civility

Notes on Civility

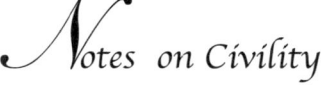

Notes on Civility

Notes on Civility

Notes on Civility

Notes on Civility

About the Author

The author is named for his ancestor, James Henry, a Scotsman who settled in Virginia, served in the Continental Congress, and loaned money to George Washington to finance the Revolutionary War. The author, who lives between Washington D.C. and Rappahannock County Virginia, has produced several documentaries and is currently working on the third and final title of the *Trilogy of Life*, titled *The Money Book*.

Printed in China